Two Great Lives
Helen Keller and Anne Sullivan

By Alan Trussell-Cullen

Illustrated by Bert Jackson

DOMINIE PRESS

Pearson Learning Group

Paperback ISBN 0-7685-1831-8
Printed in Singapore
  3 4 5 6   05

Dominie
Press
Pearson Learning Group

1-800-321-3106
www.pearsonlearning.com

Table of Contents

Chapter One

Growing Up without Sight or Sound

Helen Keller was born in Alabama on June 27, 1880. She was a lively, healthy baby, and she began to grow into a strong toddler. But shortly before she turned two, she became very ill. She had a terrible fever, and her parents thought she would die. The fever passed, but it left Helen completely blind and deaf.

Suddenly, the bright young girl had been cut off from the world.

But Helen wasn't the kind of person who gives up easily. She couldn't see or hear what was happening around her, so she explored her world by using the senses she still had.

She clung to her mother's dress and followed her around the house. She touched and smelled everything she came across. She recognized people by touching their faces and by the feel of the clothes they wore.

She would take hold of people's hands in order to find out what they were doing. In this way, she learned how to do things like knead dough and milk cows.

Helen was learning to communicate

by actions, too. She would pretend to cut a slice of bread to tell people she was hungry and wanted some bread to eat. She loved ice cream. Her family knew that when she gave a shiver, it meant Helen wanted some ice cream to eat.

But by the time Helen turned five, she knew there was a lot she was missing out on. She knew that people used their mouths to say things. But she couldn't hear anything, so she didn't know what they were saying. There were times when Helen became very angry and frustrated. She would throw tantrums, kicking and screaming in her rage.

As she grew older, she became even more frustrated. Her temper would boil over and she would throw things. Something had to be done about Helen—but what?

Her parents decided to write to the Perkins School for the Blind, in Boston, to ask for help.

The school officials wrote back. They had just the person to help Helen.

Chapter Two

Growing Up without a Family

Anne Sullivan was born in April, 1866, in a small village near Springfield, Massachusetts. She had a miserable childhood.

Her parents were very poor, and there was always trouble at home. Her father drank too much and lost his job often. Her mother suffered from tuberculosis. She died when Anne was a young child. Anne and her brother, Jimmy, were passed around from relative to relative.

At age five, Anne came down with an eye disease, and her sight began to get worse and worse.

When Anne was ten, her father could not find any other relatives to look after Anne and Jimmy, so they were sent to the state "poorhouse" in Tewksbury, Massachusetts.

This was a terrible place for children to grow up. Many of the people living there were mentally ill, or criminals, or just unfortunate people who could not survive on their own.

Jimmy was frightened at night, and Anne had to argue at length to be allowed to have his bed placed beside hers. But Jimmy was a sickly child, and he soon died. Anne was all alone in the world.

But Anne had a dream. She desperately wanted to go to school and learn. She had heard of schools for the blind, and she was sure that was where she should go.

One day, a group of people came to inspect the poorhouse. Anne ran up to the head of the group and begged to be sent to a school for the blind. A few weeks later, she heard that she was being sent to the Perkins School for the Blind.

At first, Anne found it difficult at Perkins. She was very intelligent, but she had a sharp tongue and a fiery temper. Her classmates gave her the nickname "Spitfire." However, she studied hard and graduated at the age of twenty, as class

valedictorian. She also had an operation that largely restored her sight.

But what would she do now?

The head of Perkins said he had the ideal job for her. There was a blind, deaf girl in Alabama named Helen Keller who needed her help.

Chapter Three
W-A-T-E-R

Anne arrived at Helen's home on
March 3, 1887. Anne was twenty-one,
and Helen was nearly seven.

The two did not get off to a good start.
Helen was stubborn, and she was used to
screaming and kicking and biting until

she got her own way. Anne was just as stubborn, and she wanted to be a successful teacher to the young Helen.

One of their first battles was over Helen's terrible table manners. Helen would help herself to food from other people's plates, and she insisted on eating everything with her fingers. One Monday morning, Anne decided that it was time this stopped.

When Helen reached over and tried to take food off Anne's plate, Anne stopped her. Helen flew into a rage. She began to scream and kick, and she tried to pull Anne's chair out from under her. Helen's family was so frightened by the scene that they left the room.

But Anne refused to react. She quietly closed the door and returned to the table. After a while, Helen started to wonder what was going on. Her tantrums had always worked before. What was different?

She went around the room, running her hands over all the chairs at the table and noticing they were empty. Then she came to Anne. Anne was still there, calmly eating her breakfast.

Helen didn't know what to make of this, so she sat down and started to eat her own breakfast—with her hands. Anne put a spoon in her hand. Helen threw it across the room. Anne took Helen's hand and made her pick up the spoon. Then she helped her sit down at the table again.

Helen was breathing hard. She reached out to see what this new person was doing. Anne was quietly eating her breakfast with her spoon. Helen gave a

sigh and began to eat her own breakfast—with a spoon.

Anne and Helen began to get along. Anne was firm but loving, and Helen began to trust her and enjoy her company. Together, they began to explore the world around the house.

Anne taught Helen the names for things by spelling out the letters on her hand. She gave Helen a doll and wrote D-O-L-L on her hand. She did the same with candy. At first, Helen thought this was just a game. She didn't notice any connection between the things she touched and the words Anne spelled out.

A month went by, and Helen was still not making a connection. Then one morning, Anne took Helen to the water pump. Anne pushed the handle, and cold water gushed out over Helen's hand.

While the water was still running, Anne wrote *W-A-T-E-R* on Helen's other hand.

Suddenly, Helen was fascinated. For the first time, she understood that words were names for things. Eager for more, she got Anne to write the word *water* on her hand several times. Then she touched the pump and got Anne to write the word *pump* on her hand. Then she ran to the fence and got Anne to write *fence*.

Then Helen stopped. She touched Anne and asked her to write her name. Anne wrote on her hand: *T-E-A-C-H-E-R*.

Chapter Four

Anne Helps Helen Discover the World

After this, Helen never looked back. Within weeks, she knew more than 300 words. She was now driven by a desire to learn as much as she could.

Anne began to teach Helen to read and write using Braille. Braille is a system of

raised bumps on paper. Each letter of the
alphabet has a different pattern of bumps,
so someone running their fingers over
the bumps can "read" the letters. At last,
Helen could read books!

Helen also began to learn how to "hear"
what people were saying by placing her
fingers lightly on the speaker's lips and

throat. Helen was doing so well that Anne decided she was ready to go to school.

In 1888, Anne took Helen to Boston so she could attend the Perkins School for the Blind. Anne went to school with Helen and continued to help her with her studies. Helen was even learning to speak, and so, in 1894, Anne took her to the Wright-Humason School for the Deaf, in New York.

Chapter Five

Anne Helps the World Discover Helen

Helen was becoming an excellent scholar. She went on to Radcliffe College, where, with Anne's support, she graduated with honors in 1904.

While still at college, Helen started writing. At first she wrote articles for magazines. Then she wrote her autobiography, *The Story of My Life*. The book was an immediate success and earned enough money for Helen to buy her own house.

By this time, Helen was famous. People everywhere were amazed by the way she had triumphed over adversity. She traveled around the world, giving speeches and meeting famous people.

But Helen was always grateful for all the help Anne and others had given her. She began to think about how she could help others. She spoke out about the injustices in the world around her. It wasn't fair that so many people were sick and poor and yet were given so little help. It wasn't fair the way women were treated as inferior. She became a suffragette, and spoke out for equal

rights for women and better pay for poor working people. She spoke out against war and campaigned for peace.

But she also worked tirelessly throughout her life to help those who were blind and those who were both blind and deaf.

Anne remained by Helen's side, helping her with her speeches and her writing. But Anne was gaining attention and fame, too. People began to recognize her, not just as the person who had devoted her life to Helen Keller, but as a great American teacher in her own right.

Anne and Helen shared many awards and triumphs. In 1955, a documentary film about Helen's life, *Helen Keller in Her Story*, won an Oscar at the Academy of Motion Picture Arts and Sciences awards ceremony. A play about

Helen and Anne, called *The Miracle Worker*, became a Broadway hit. It was later made into a prize-winning movie in which the actors who played Anne and Helen, Anne Bancroft and Patty Duke, both won Oscars for their performances.

Anne remained by Helen's side, right up to Anne's death in 1936. Both women knew how much they owed each other. Anne gave her whole life over to supporting Helen and helping her become a shining example of courage and determination.

But in return, Helen gave Anne a deep sense of family and stability that she had never known. Together, their achievements are intertwined. Helen Keller and Anne Sullivan—two great lives.